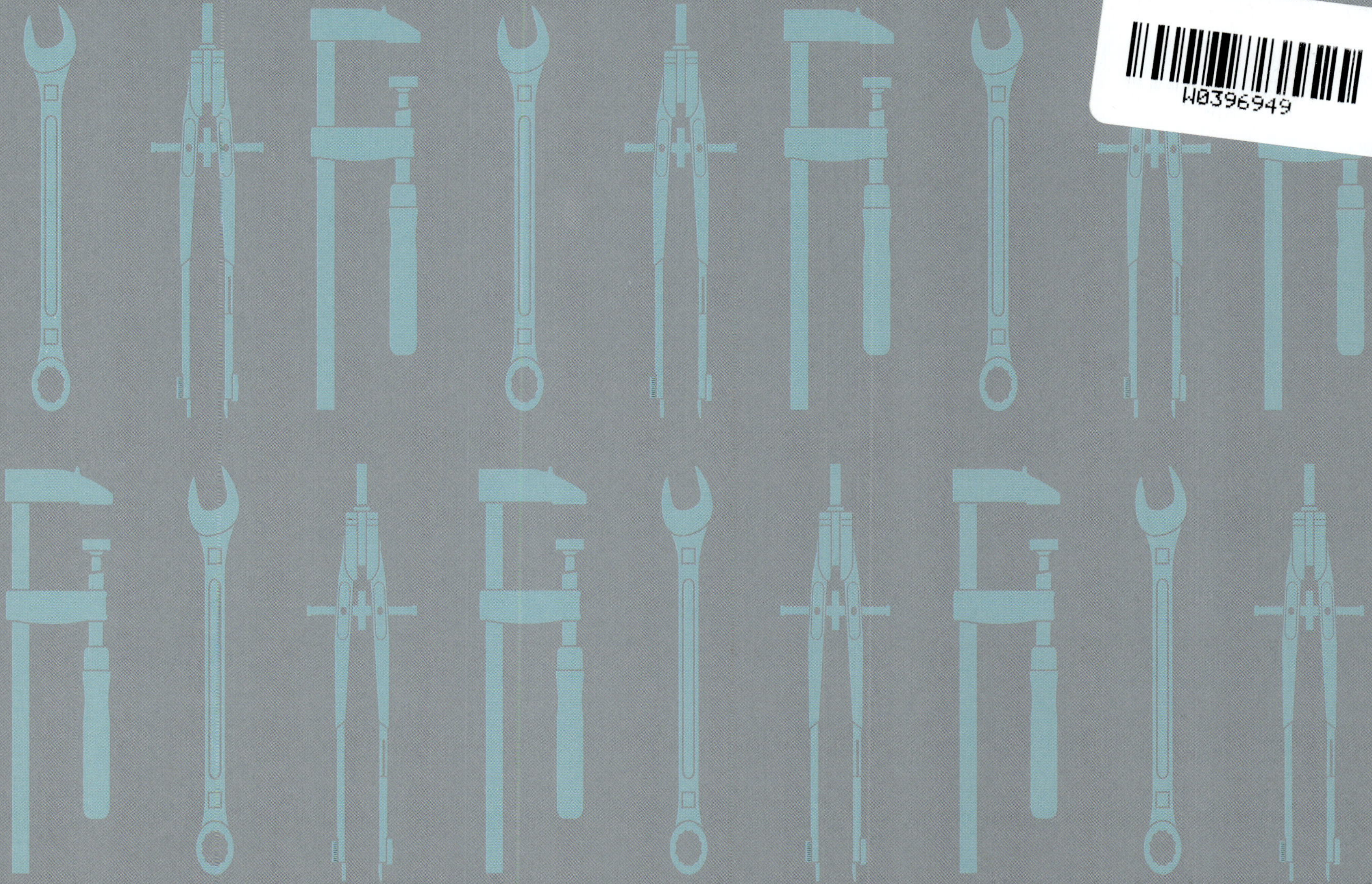

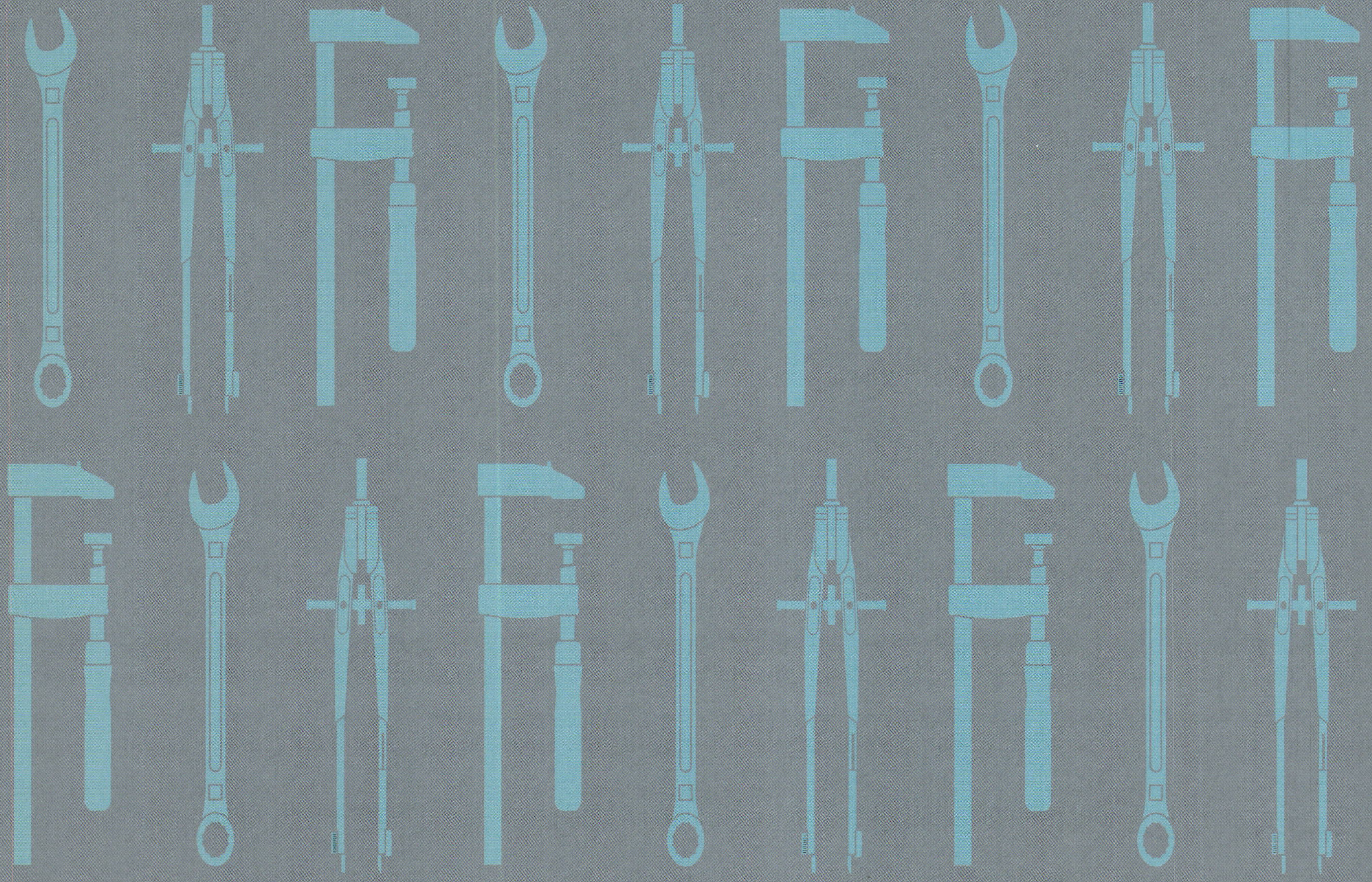

KARL LANG

BRIDGES PANORAMA

Text by Imre Török

EDITIONPANORAMA

BRÜCKENBETRACHTUNGEN

Alle unsere Sinne bilden Brücken zu der Welt um uns. Die Augen spannen dabei den Bogen zur Schönheit von Farben, Linien und Formen, sie erlauben es uns, die faszinierende Vielfalt der uns umgebenden Bilder im Kopf, in der Fantasie erneut entstehen zu lassen.

Mit jedem Augenaufschlag, das Reich der fließenden Träume verlassend, betreten wir die Brücke des Lichts. Schreiten auf den Strahlen, die in die Augen fallen, gleiten auf dieser lichten Verbindung zu Buchstaben oder Bauwerken, betrachten Nahes und Fernes, Festes und Lebendiges.

Manchmal betrachten und bewundern wir die geschwungenen Bögen einer Brücke. Über dem breiten Fluss, über dem tiefen Abgrund. Entdecken ein Brückchen, zwischen zwei Häusern nur, oder wir stehen vor großartigen technischen Konstruktionen, welche Buchten und Meerengen überspannen. Stets, so scheint es, werden dabei mehr als nur zwei getrennte Orte miteinander verbunden. Brücken wissen Geschichten zu erzählen.

Als Vincent van Gogh 1888 nach Arles in der Provence kam, empfingen ihn sowohl „freundliches Licht" als auch südliches Lodern der Sonne. In dieser Aura der Farb- und Lichtspiele malte van Gogh mehrere Versionen des berühmten Gemäldes „Die Brücke von Langlois bei Arles." Eine pittoreske Zugbrücke, über die in einer Version eine kleine Pferdekarre fährt, während unten am Wasser bunt gekleidete Wäscherinnen ihre Arbeit verrichten. Die gesamte Komposition aus Gelb, Orange, Blau und Rot, Rosa,

VIEW OF BRIDGES

All our senses build bridges to the world around us. The eyes span the arch to the beauty of colours, lines and shapes, they enable us to recreate in our minds and in our imagination the fascinating variety of the images that surround us.

Every time we open our eyes, leaving the realm of flowing dreams, we tread the bridge of light – tread the beams which meet our eyes, glide this tenuous connection to letters or building works, view the near and far, the immovable and the living.

Sometimes we look at and admire the vaulting arches of a bridge, spanning a broad river or bottomless abyss. We discover a small bridge, perhaps only between two houses, or we stand before enormous architectural constructions spanning whole bays or sea narrows. Always, it seems, they do more than simply connecting two separate locations. Bridges have many stories to tell.

When Vincent van Gogh arrived in Arles in Provence in 1888, he was received by both "friendly light" and the southern glow of the sun. In this aura of colour and interplay of light, van Gogh painted several versions of the famous painting "The Langlois Bridge at Arles." A picturesque drawbridge, over which in one version a small horse buggy has just crossed the bridge, while at the water's edge below, brightly-dressed washerwomen go about their work. The whole composition of yellow, orange, blue and red, pink and green radiates the rhythmical interruptions of life between the sky and the water, in a landscape saturated by

RÉFLEXIONS SUR LES PONTS

Tous nos sens forment des ponts avec le monde qui nous environne. Nos yeux, par exemple, enjambent l'abîme qui nous sépare de la beauté des couleurs, des lignes et des formes. Grâce à eux, nous pouvons recréer dans notre tête, notre imagination, la fascinante variété des images qui nous entourent.

Chaque fois que nous ouvrons les yeux, que nous quittons le monde des rêves inaccessibles, nous entrons dans le monde de la lumière en empruntant le pont jeté par nos organes de la vue. Notre perception capte les rayons qui glissent sur nos pupilles pour entamer un voyage qui nous amène à découvrir le monde des lettres, des édifices, de toutes les choses lointaines et proches, immobiles et vivantes.

Nous prenons parfois le temps de contempler et d'admirer l'élégance des arches d'un pont au-dessus d'un large fleuve ou d'un profond abîme. Il nous est déjà arrivé à tous de découvrir un modeste petit pont reliant deux maisons seulement ou de tomber en admiration devant ces gigantesques ouvrages d'art tendus au-dessus de baies et de détroits de mer. On pourrait penser, du moins c'est ce qu'il semble, que les ponts se contentent de relier concrètement deux lieux séparés, mais les ponts sont beaucoup plus que cela : ils racontent aussi des histoires.

Lorsque Vincent van Gogh arrive en Provence en 1888, plus précisément à Arles, il est accueilli par une «lumière amicale» et le flamboiement méridional du soleil. Plongé dans cette aura de jeux de couleurs et de lumières, van

CONTEMPLANDO PUENTES

Todos nuestros sentidos forman puentes entre nuestro entorno y nuestro yo. Nuestros ojos, por ejemplo, salvan el abismo que separa nuestro ego del bello mundo de los colores, las líneas y las formas. De esta forma nos permiten recrear de nuevo en nuestro cerebro, en nuestra fantasía, la fascinante variedad de las imágenes que nos rodean.

Todos nos tomamos de vez en cuando un momento para contemplar y admirar los dinámicos arcos de un puente sobre un ancho río o un proceloso abismo. Todos hemos descubierto en ocasiones alguno de esos modestos puentecillos que sólo comunican dos casas. Y, por último, todos nos hemos parado asombrados ante esas gigantescas construcciones técnicas que cruzan bahías y estrechos marinos.

Se podría pensar, al menos así parece, que se trata de la mera conexión física entre dos lugares separados; pero los puentes pueden hacer mucho más: los puentes narran historias.

Cuando Vincent van Gogh llegó a la Provence procedente de Arles en el año 1888, se sintió agradablemente acogido tanto por la "amable luz" como por el meridional ardor del sol. Inmerso en aquella aura de luminosos juegos cromáticos, van Gogh encontró la inspiración para pintar varias versiones de su célebre cuadro "El puente de Langlois en Arles". El motivo de esa serie era un pintoresco puente levadizo sobre el que en una de las versiones cruza un pequeño carro de caballos mientras que en el plano inferior de la imagen un grupo de mujeres de coloridos trajes lava la ropa en la orilla. El conjunto de la composición en los colores

OSSERVAZIONI SUI PONTI

Tutti i nostri sensi costruiscono ponti sul mondo attorno a noi. Gli occhi tendono l'arco verso la bellezza di colori, linee e forme e ci permettono ancora una volta di formare nella nostra mente con la fantasia la molteplicità delle immagini che ci circondano.

Ad ogni sguardo, lasciando fluire il regno dei sogni, mettiamo piede sul ponte della luce. Camminiamo sui raggi che penetrano nei nostri occhi, scivoliamo su questo luminoso collegamento con le lettere o gli edifici, osserviamo ciò che ci è vicino e lontano, ciò che è fermo e ciò che vive.

A volte ci soffermiamo ad osservare ed ammirare gli archi ricurvi di un ponte su di un ampio fiume o un profondo strapiombo. Scopriamo un ponticello solitario tra due case, oppure davanti a noi si ergono grandi costruzioni tecniche protese sopra insenature e stretti. Sempre, così sembra, sono più di due luoghi separati ad essere collegati. I ponti sanno raccontare storie.

Quando nel 1888 Vincent van Gogh arrivò ad Arles in Provenza ad accoglierlo c'erano quella "luce amabile" e l'arsura del sole meridionale. In quest'aura di giochi di luce e colore van Gogh dipinse diverse versioni della famosa opera "Il ponte di Langlois ad Arles." Un pittoresco ponte levatoio su cui, in una delle versioni dell'opera, passa un piccolo carro tirato da un cavallo mentre, più in basso sull'acqua, le lavandaie dagli abiti variopinti sono intente al lavoro. Dall'intera composizione in giallo, arancio, azzurro e rosso, rosa e verde promanano le interruzioni ritmiche

Grün strahlt die rhythmischen Unterbrechungen des Lebens zwischen Himmel und Wasser aus, in einer lichtgesättigten Landschaft. Und das Gemälde verbindet doch die Elemente, die Natur, die Menschen, die einfache Technik der Zugbrücke, die Farben und das Licht zu einer wunderbaren Einheit. „Mich entzückt immer noch der Zauber der dann und wann hereinhuschenden Kindheitserinnerungen, einer Sehnsucht nach dem Unendlichen ...“, notierte Vincent van Gogh in Arles.

In einem kreativen Schreibkurs sollten Kinder die Brücke als Metapher für die Bögen der Spannung in einer Geschichte verstehen lernen. Zunächst hieß es, Brücken zu bauen. Aus dem Einfachsten, was sich am Waldrand finden ließ, sollten drei Gruppen nach eigener Vorstellung jeweils eine kleine Brücke errichten.

Es war beeindruckend, mit welcher inneren Anteilnahme und forschender Begeisterung die Kinder ans Werk gingen. In allen Fällen bildeten gebogene, ineinandergeflochtene Zweige den Bogen. Bei der weiteren Gestaltung und Ausschmückung entstanden jedoch drei ganz unterschiedliche Versionen. Die Blumenbrücke leuchtete mit prächtig gelbem Löwenzahn. Bei einer anderen Konstruktion dienten Stücke abgefallener Baumrinde und Moos als Belag. Die dritte Gruppe hat es geschafft, den Belag aus Zweigen und Blättern mit grauem Kiesel zu bedecken, sodass eine steinerne Brückenminiatur entstanden war.

Auch die ersten begehbaren Überbrückungen in der Menschheitsgeschichte wurden simpel aus Baumstämmen und Ästen errichtet, oder man flocht aus Lianen, Schilf, Bambus hängende Pfade, die schwankend durch die

light. And the painting itself connects the elements, nature, people, the simple technology of the drawbridge, the colour and the light into a wonderful unity. “I am still delighted by the magic of the fleeting, occasional childhood memories, a longing for the infinite ...”, wrote Vincent van Gogh in Arles.

In a creative writing course, children were to learn to understand the bridge as a metaphor for the arches of tension in a story. The first thing to do was to build bridges. From the simplest materials that can be found at the edge of the forest, three groups were to each build a small bridge according to their own design.

It was impressive to see with what genuine interest and inquisitive enthusiasm the children went about the task. In all designs, the arch was formed by bent and interwoven branches. In the further construction and embellishment however, three quite different versions were created. The flower bridge shone with rich yellow dandelions. In another construction, pieces of fallen tree bark and moss were used as the covering. The third group succeeded in covering the carriageway of branches and leaves with grey gravel, producing a miniature stone bridge.

The first passable bridges in human history also consisted simply of tree trunks and boughs, or suspended pathways woven from lianas, reeds or bamboo, leading their swinging way through inaccessible terrain. Four thousand years ago, simple suspension bridges were known and used in China and India. Even in ancient times, floating pontoon bridges enable the crossing of rivers. These consisted of boats lashed together, with a carriageway fitted over the

Gogh trouve ici l'inspiration pour peindre plusieurs versions de son célèbre tableau «Le pont de Langlois» dont le motif est un pont-levis pittoresque sur lequel passe une charrette tirée par des chevaux, tandis qu'en bas, au bord du canal, des lavandières vêtues de tenues colorées s'affairent. Cette œuvre dont la composition est dominée par le jaune, l'orange, le bleu, le rouge, le rose et le vert est une métaphore des interruptions rythmiques de la vie, un reflet finalement du rapport entre le ciel et l'eau dans un paysage saturé de lumière. Ce tableau parvient à amalgamer les éléments, la nature, les êtres humains, la simplicité technique du pont-levis, les couleurs et la lumière, pour créer une merveilleuse unité. «Je m'extasie encore sur l'effet magique des souvenirs d'enfance. De ces souvenirs qui me reviennent à la mémoire de temps en temps, alimentant ma nostalgie de l'infini …» a écrit Vincent van Gogh à Arles.

A l'occasion d'un cours d'écriture créative, on a proposé à des enfants de considérer le pont comme une métaphore pour les arcs formés par la tension narrative d'une histoire. On leur a d'abord demandé de construire un pont avec les choses les plus simples qu'ils pourraient trouver à la lisière d'un bois puis on a suggéré à chacun des trois groupes formés de construire un pont tout en suivant leur imagination.

L'intérêt manifesté par tous les enfants pour cette tâche mais aussi leur enthousiasme investigateur étaient impressionnants à voir. Bien que les trois groupes aient construit un pont en utilisant des branches pliées et entrelacées, leurs travaux ont abouti à la création de trois versions fondamentalement différentes en raison de l'arrangement et de la décoration choisis. Le premier pont était un ouvrage floral

amarillo, naranja, azul, rojo, rosa y verde se convierte en una metáfora de las rítmicas interrupciones que experimenta la vida. Un reflejo en fin de la relación entre el cielo y el agua en un paisaje saturado de luz. Esta pintura logra amalgamar los elementos, la naturaleza, los seres humanos, la sencilla técnica del puente levadizo, los colores y la luz formando así finalmente una maravillosa unidad. "Me sigue extasiando el encanto de los recuerdos de la infancia. De esos recuerdos que de vez en cuando se me vienen a la mente y consiguen despertar de nuevo en mí la añoranza por lo eterno...", escribía Vincent van Gogh en Arles.

En una ocasión, en un curso de creatividad literaria, se propuso a los niños que entendieran la figura de un puente como la metáfora del arco que forma la tensión narrativa de una historia. Para empezar se les pidió que intentaran construir un puente con las cosas más simples que se encontraran en los bordes de un bosque. Se les dividió en tres grupos y se les sugirió que cada uno de ellos construyera un puente siguiendo su imaginación.

Fue impresionante ver con que pasión investigadora y con que motivación los niños pusieron manos a la obra. Aunque en todos los casos los niños formaron los arcos con ramas combadas y entrelazadas, las diferencias entre las tres versiones resultaron notables tanto en su elaboración ulterior como en su decoración. El primer ejemplo, un puente de flores, lucía una esplendorosa ornamentación de amarillos dientes de león. En la siguiente construcción los niños utilizaron pedazos de corteza caída y musgo para dotar a su puente de un revestimiento. El tercer grupo incluso llegó a cubrir con grava gris el "pavimento" de ramas y hojas, de

della vita che scorre tra il cielo e l'acqua in un paesaggio saturo di luce. E il dipinto fonde tra loro gli elementi, la natura, le persone, il rudimentale ingranaggio del ponte levatoio, i colori e la luce in una magnifica unità. "Mi affascina sempre la magia dei ricordi che di tanto in tanto emergono dall'infanzia, da quella nostalgia d'infinito ...", scriveva nei suoi appunti Vincent van Gogh ad Arles.

In un corso di scrittura creativa i ragazzi dovevano imparare a vedere il ponte come archi che tendono ad una storia. Per prima cosa bisogna imparare a costruire un ponte partendo dal più semplice, uno come quelli che si trovano alla fine di un bosco. I tre gruppi di ragazzi dovevano realizzare un piccolo ponte come a loro più piaceva.

La partecipazione interiore e l'entusiasmo per la ricerca con cui si misero al lavoro era impressionante. In tutti i casi l'arco risultò costituito da rami curvati ed intrecciati. Nell'altro lavoro e nella decorazione furono create tre versioni completamente diverse. Il ponte di fiori splendeva nel giallo squillante del dente di leone. Un'altra costruzione era ricoperta di pezzi di corteccia caduta e muschio. Il terzo gruppo riuscì a coprire di ciottoli grigi lo strato di rami e foglie creando così un ponte in miniatura con le pietre.

Anche i primi valichi praticabili della storia dell'umanità venivano costruiti semplicemente con tronchi d'albero e rami, oppure con liane intrecciate, canne palustri e percorsi in bambù appeso che consentivano di attraversare oscillando i punti impraticabili. Quattromila anni prima in Cina ed India si utilizzavano semplici ponti sospesi. Già nell'antichità i ponti di barconi consentivano di attraversare i fiumi. Le barche venivano assicurate tra loro e su di esse

Unwegbarkeit führten. Vor viertausend Jahren kannte und benutzte man in China und Indien einfache Hängebrücken. Bereits in der Antike ermöglichten schwimmende Pontonbrücken die Überquerung von Flüssen. Boote wurden aneinander getäut, über sie wurde ein Steg montiert. Die architektonische Kunstfertigkeit, Bögen aus Stein von Pfeiler zu Pfeiler zu errichten, erreichte im antiken Römischen Reich eine für die damalige Zeit bewundernswerte Perfektion.

Brücken wurden dabei nicht nur über Gewässer geschlagen, Wasser floss auch über die Brücke. Solche Aquädukte, wasserführende Brücken, zählen zu den bedeutendsten Bauwerken der geschichtlichen Hochkulturen. Die Anhöhen und Täler überquerenden Wasserleitungen, diese Steinkanäle auf gewölbten Bogenstellungen, die manchmal auch mehrstöckig gebaut wurden, führten frisches Quellwasser in die Städte. Ein imposanter Zeuge antiker Brückenbaukunst ist der aus Abertausenden von Steinblöcken erbaute Aquädukt im spanischen Segovia. Das in der Römerzeit errichtete Meisterwerk fortlaufender steinerner Bögen, mit über 700 Meter Länge und beinahe 30 Meter Höhe, versorgte noch bis vor wenigen Jahrzehnten die Einwohner Segovias mit Wasser.

Natürlich stehen Ingenieuren und Architekten zwei Jahrtausende später atemberaubend andere Möglichkeiten an Werkstoffen, Technik und physikalischen Erkenntnissen zur Verfügung, um in berauschend schöne Sphären und technische Dimensionen des modernen Brückenbaus vorzustoßen. Zu Beginn unseres Jahrtausends wurde die zur Zeit größte Brücke der Welt in Japan fertiggestellt. Die

top. The architectural virtuosity of erecting arches of stone from pillar to pillar, reached an astounding perfection for the time in the ancient Roman Empire.

Bridges were erected not only over water, but also to carry water. Such aqueducts are amongst the most notable building works of ancient developed cultures. These waterways crossing hills and valleys, these stone channels on vaulted arches, which were sometimes also built in several storeys, brought fresh spring water to the towns and cities. An imposing testament to the ancient art of bridge-building is the aqueduct in Segovia in Spain, which is constructed of thousands and thousands of stone blocks. Erected in Roman times, this masterpiece of continuous stone arches is over 2,300 ft. long and almost 100 ft. high, and continued to supply the residents of Segovia with water until only a few decades ago.

Today of course, 2,000 years later, modern engineers and architects have at their disposal a breathtaking range of other possibilities when it comes to materials, technology and knowledge of physics, in order to advance the modern art of bridge-building with amazingly beautiful designs and astounding technical dimensions. At the beginning of this century, currently the largest bridge in the world was completed in Japan. The Akashi Kaikyo Suspension Bridge has a span of almost 6,600 ft. The frequent danger of earthquakes presented enormous challenges to the builders. Vibration dampers had to be installed into the two pylons, the steel towers almost 1,000 ft. high supporting the bridge, and they have already demonstrated that they can absorb severe earth tremors.

avec des pissenlits d'un jaune superbe. Pour le deuxième en revanche, les enfants avaient utilisé des morceaux d'écorce qu'ils avaient trouvés par terre ainsi que de la mousse pour couvrir le pont. Le troisième groupe a réussi quant à lui à couvrir le revêtement de branches et de feuilles avec des graviers gris afin de créer un pont de pierre en miniature.
Les premiers ponts praticables également dans l'histoire de l'humanité étaient tous des ouvrages rudimentaires faits de troncs d'arbre et de branches ou encore de lianes, de joncs et de bambous tressés qui formaient une passerelle suspendue vacillante au-dessus d'un abîme ou d'une rivière infranchissable. Les Chinois et les Indiens, il y a quatre mille ans, connaissaient et utilisaient de simples ponts suspendus. Dans l'Antiquité déjà, on franchissait des rivières par de véritables pontons flottants formés par des bateaux amarrés les uns aux autres sur lesquels une passerelle était posée. Plus tard encore, dans l'Empire Romain antique, l'habileté des architectes à construire des arches en pierre d'un pilier à l'autre atteint une perfection admirable compte tenu des conditions et des circonstances de l'époque.
Des ponts étaient érigés non seulement pour franchir des fleuves et des rivières, mais aussi, bien souvent, pour acheminer l'eau. Ces aqueducs, véritables ponts d'adduction d'eau, comptent sans aucun doute parmi les ouvrages d'ingénierie les plus significatifs de l'architecture ayant été produits par les hautes civilisations anciennes. Ces conduites d'eau qui franchissent montagnes et vallées, ces canaux de pierre reposant sur d'impressionnantes rangées d'arches, parfois superposées, acheminaient jusqu'aux villes l'eau fraîche de sources lointaines. L'Aqueduc de Ségovie en Es-

forma que obtuvieron un puente de piedra en miniatura.
También los primeros vados artificiales transitables de la historia de la humanidad fueron formados con medios sencillos como troncos de árboles y ramas. Más tarde se empezaron a trenzar lianas, juncos y cañas de bambú para formar pasos colgantes, que oscilando de acá para allá, conducían a través de lo intransitable. Ya hace unos cuatro mil años se conocían y se usaban en China e India puentes colgantes de sencilla factura. También en la antigüedad se hacía posible el traspaso de corrientes fluviales a través de puentes flotantes de pontones: normalmente se amarraban con estachas largas filas de botes por los costados y, una vez en el agua, se montaba sobre los botes una pasarela. Más tarde aún, durante el Imperio Romano, el arte arquitectónico de erigir arcos de piedra entre pilares alcanzó una perfección realmente admirable si se tienen en cuenta las condiciones y circunstancias de aquella época.
Los puentes no sólo se levantaban por encima de las aguas, sino que también se construían para transportar el líquido elemento. Los acueductos se cuentan sin duda entre los más significativos monumentos arquitectónicos que han producido las civilizaciones históricas. Estas conducciones de agua –impresionantes canales de piedra que descansaban sobre impresionantes filas de arcos y que a veces contaban con varios pisos de altura– superaban montañas y salvaban valles para transportar hasta las ciudades las frescas aguas de lejanos manantiales. El Acueducto de Segovia, para cuya construcción se emplearon miles y miles de bloques de piedra, constituye un impresionante documento del grado de perfección al que llegó el arte de la construc-

veniva montato un pontile. L'abilità architettonica di costruire archi in pietra da pilone a pilone raggiunse nell'antica Roma una perfezione ammirevole per l'epoca.
Ma i ponti a quei tempi non venivano solo lambiti dalle acque che vi scorrevano anche sopra. Questi acquedotti, ponti che trasportavano acqua, sono tra le opere più significative delle grandi civiltà della storia. Le tubature che attraversavano alture e valli, questi canali in pietra su postazioni a volta che potevano anche essere costruite su di più piani, rifornivano le città d'acqua fresca di sorgente. Un imponente testimone dell'architettura dell'antichità è l'acquedotto di Segovia in Spagna, costruito con parecchie migliaia di blocchi di pietra. Il capolavoro costruito in epoca romana costruito su file d'archi in pietra, con oltre 700 metri di lunghezza e quasi 30 metri d'altezza, riforniva d'acqua gli abitanti della città spagnola fino a pochi decenni fa.
Sono trascorsi due millenni ed oggi naturalmente ingegneri e architetti hanno altri mezzi tecnologici, diversi materiali e conoscenze fisiche a disposizione per catturare la bellezza e definire le dimensioni tecniche della costruzione moderna dei ponti. All'inizio del nostro millennio venne realizzato in Giappone il ponte all'epoca più grande al mondo. Il ponte sospeso Akashi Kaikyo ha una campata di quasi due chilometri. Il frequente rischio di terremoti poneva delle sfide enormi ai costruttori perciò nei due piloni, le torri in acciaio che sostenevano il ponte di quasi 300 metri d'altezza, vennero inseriti degli elementi ammortizzanti la cui funzione, già dimostrata, è quella d'attutire le gravi scosse telluriche.

Akashi Kaikyo Hängebrücke hat eine Spannweite von nahezu zwei Kilometern. Die häufige Erdbebengefahr stellte die Konstrukteure vor gewaltige Herausforderungen. So wurden in die zwei Pylone, die Brücke tragende Stahltürme von fast 300 Meter Höhe, Schwingungsdämpfer eingebaut. Sie haben bereits bewiesen, dass sie schwere Erdstöße abfedern können.
Zurück zu den kindlichen Brückenbauern des Schreibkurses, ihrem Suchen nach Material, ihren konzentrierten Überlegungen beim Bauen. Wie beeindruckend, das schöpferisch Verbindende der emsigen kleinen Hände, der gemeinsamen Ideen und des neu entstandenen, verbindenden Bogens inmitten der Gruppen. Um so spannender wurde die Frage, was für Geschichten den Kindern zum Thema Brücke einfallen würden. Und es war überraschend, dass aus der kindlichen Fantasie viel seltener das imposant Schöne oder die nützlich verbindende Funktion einer Brücke aufs Papier gelangt war. Viel öfter thematisierten sie die Gefahr beim Überqueren eines Gewässers. Mutproben waren angesagt, von schwankenden Brücken, einstürzendem Geländer ging die Rede. Aber stets wurde das ins Wasser gefallene Kind gerettet, die Brücke wieder begehbar gemacht.
Ja, die Verbindung, welche uns faszinierende und erhabene Wege über die Gefahr spannt, lässt ein Kribbeln nicht verschwinden, ob die Verbindung auch wirklich trägt.
Trotzdem lieben wir die Magie des Überquerens, des Überwindens. Schauen begeistert aus dem Fenster, während der Zug über schwindelnd hohe Viadukte die Täler der Bergwelt passiert. Kurbeln das Wagenfester herunter,

Back to the young bridge-builders of the writing course, their search for materials, their concentrated considerations when building. How impressive, the creative activity of the busy small hands, the joint ideas and the newly-created connecting arch amongst the groups. All the more exciting the question of what stories would occur to the children on the subject of bridges. And it was surprising how infrequently the imposing beauty or the utilitarian connecting function of a bridge found its way onto paper from the children's imagination. The more frequent subject was the potential danger in crossing a stretch of water. Tests of courage were recommended, while the talk was of swaying bridges or collapsing railings. But the child who fell into the water was always rescued, and the bridge made passable again.
Yes, the connection which offers us fascinating and elevated ways above danger still make our nerves tingle with anxiety as to whether the bridge will bear our weight.
Nevertheless we still love the magic of the crossing, of overcoming natural obstacles. We peer eagerly out of the window, as the train crosses mountain valleys on dizzyingly high viaducts, winding the carriage window down to let in the fresh sea air and watch ships passing by below us, such as when crossing the majestic Öresund Bridge between Denmark and Sweden, one of the largest construction works in Europe. And how enchanting are the garlands of light of a bridge at night, the sweeping lines over the water and its shimmering, bright reflection in the dark waters. Arches dotted with light above small streams of an old town with its winding alleyways, or a picturesque park. Or spher-

pagne, dont la construction a nécessité des milliers et des milliers de blocs en pierre de taille, témoigne de manière extraordinaire du degré de perfection auquel étaient parvenus les bâtisseurs de ponts dans l'Antiquité. Ce chef-d'œuvre érigé sous l'Empire romain, cet ouvrage formé de rangées d'arches continues sur deux étages, s'étire sur plus de 700 m de long et se dresse à presque 30 m du sol à son point culminant. Jusqu'il y a quelques décennies, il était encore en service et approvisionnait en eau la ville de Ségovie.

Deux mille ans plus tard, les ingénieurs et les architectes ont naturellement à leur disposition un éventail fantastique d'options – de nouveaux matériaux, de nouvelles techniques et de meilleures connaissances des fondements physiques de la construction – qui leur permettent de pousser plus loin dans les sphères de la beauté et les dimensions techniques de la construction moderne de ponts. Au début de notre millénaire, le plus grand pont moderne de l'époque est inauguré au Japon, à savoir le pont suspendu d'«Akashi Kaikyo» dont l'envergure atteint presque deux kilomètres. Les tremblements de terre fréquents constituent un risque qui a obligé les concepteurs à relever des défis de taille. Ils ont ainsi prévu de gigantesques dispositifs amortisseurs dans les deux piliers qui soutiennent le pont afin d'assurer des amplitudes de mouvement. Ces tours d'acier de presque 300 m de haut ont démontré dans la pratique qu'elles pouvaient amortir des séismes de grande intensité.

C'est évident : nous ne pouvons pas nous défaire d'une certaine nervosité lorsque nous empruntons ces voies fascinantes et élevées, nous nous demandons toujours si le pont va vraiment tenir.

ción de puentes en la antigüedad. Esta obra maestra que fue construida durante el dominio romano y que está compuesta por arcos de piedra que llegan a alcanzar más de 700 metros de longitud y casi 30 metros de altura, todavía siguió llevando agua a Segovia hasta hace pocas décadas.

Naturalmente que, dos mil años más tarde, los arquitectos e ingenieros disponen de un fantástico espectro de opciones –nuevos materiales, nuevas técnicas y un profundo conocimiento de los fundamentos científicos de la construcción– para experimentar con las nuevas dimensiones técnicas de la edificación de puentes y de paso adentrarse en esferas estéticas de una belleza que quita el aliento. Justo a principios del actual milenio fue inaugurado en Japón el mayor puente de la actualidad. El puente colgante "Akashi Kaikyo" tiene una luz arquitectónica de casi dos kilómetros. El riesgo que suponen los frecuentes movimientos sísmicos obligó a los constructores a superar tremendos retos. Por ejemplo, fue necesario integrar amortiguadores de la vibración en los dos pilones que sostienen el puente. Ambas gigantescas torres de acero de casi 300 metros de altura ya han demostrado en la práctica que son capaces de amortiguar intensos seísmos.

Sí, está claro: todos sentimos un extraño hormigueo en el estómago al acceder a estas fascinantes y elevadas vías. Todos nos preguntamos si la unión soportará sus cargas.

Y a pesar de ello, todos amamos la magia que supone cruzar al otro lado, superar el abismo. Todos contemplamos con grandes ojos el paisaje desde la ventana mientras nuestro tren traspasa valles y supera montañas sobre viaductos de vertiginosa altura. Y es por eso que bajamos entusias-

Ma torniamo alla costruzione dei ponti con i ragazzi del corso di scrittura e alla loro ricerca del materiale, alle loro concentrate riflessioni durante il lavoro di costruzione. Com'è impressionante il lavoro creativo di collegamento delle piccole mani operose, la fusione tra le idee e l'unione –l'arco- formato dal gruppo. Che tipo di storia avrebbero inventato i ragazzi sul tema del ponte? La domanda era avvincente. Strano però che la fantasia infantile solo ben più raramente descrivesse sulla carta la bellezza maestosa o la funzione d'utilità di un ponte. Molto più spesso i ragazzi preferirono parlare del pericolo d'attraversare un corso d'acqua. Annunciavano prove di coraggio nell'affrontare ponti oscillanti, descrivevano parapetti che crollavano. Però il bimbo caduto in acqua si salvava sempre e il ponte tornava ad essere agibile.

Sì, il tratto che collega tra loro percorsi sublimi ed affascinanti non annulla gli altri movimenti impercettibili, se l'unione è profonda e reale.

Però amiamo sempre la magia dell'attraversamento, del superamento. Il guardare entusiasti dalla finestra mentre il treno percorre su altezze vertiginose le valli di un paesaggio montano. Ci piace abbassare il finestrino, fare entrare l'aria fresca del mare e vedere le navi che passano sotto, ad esempio durante la traversata del maestoso ponte Öresund tra la Danimarca e la Svezia, una delle più grandi opere edili mai realizzate in Europa. E come magiche appaiono le ghirlande di luce di un ponte illuminato di notte, le linee arcuate sull'acqua e il tremolante e variopinto riflesso sull'acqua nera che scorre. Gli archi punteggiati di luce sui piccoli corsi d'acqua di una città storica con i suoi angoli o

lassen den frischen Seewind herein und sehen Schiffe unter uns hindurchfahren, zum Beispiel bei der Fahrt auf der majestätischen Öresundbrücke zwischen Dänemark und Schweden, einem der größten technischen Bauwerke in Europa. Und wie bezaubernd wirken die Lichtgirlanden einer Brücke in der Nacht, die geschwungenen Linien über dem Wasser und ihre zitternde, bunte Widerspiegelung auf dem dunklen Dahinströmen. Lichtbetupfte Bögen über kleine Wasserläufe einer verwinkelten Altstadt, eines malerischen Parks. Oder sphärisch kühne Linien zwischen entfernten Ufern, das schäumende Meer überragend.

Stets erzählen Brücken in bunter Bildersprache. Erzählen oft romantisch aus fernöstlichen Gärten und stillen Landschaften, flüstern auch von Flaneuren, verliebten Paaren am Seineufer in Paris oder an der Donau, unter den Lichtern der Kettenbrücke in Budapest. Und Brücken singen mit den Gondolieren auf Venedigs Lagunen. Doch die Bauwerke der bezaubernden Bögen können auch andere Erinnerungen wecken.

Die anmutige venezianische Seufzerbrücke aus weißem Kalkstein erinnert an bedrückende Zeiten. Verurteilte sollen im 17. Jahrhundert über die Seufzerbrücke ins Gefängnis geführt worden sein und erblickten beim Überschreiten der Lagune für lange Zeit oder für immer das letzte Mal das Licht der Freiheit.

Die elegante „Stari Most“ (Alte Brücke) in Bosnien-Herzegowina war 450 Jahre lang die schönste Brücke auf dem Balkan. Sie verband Handelswege von der Adria ins Landesinnere. Die Brückenwächter hießen in der Landessprache „Mostari“, sie gaben der Stadt Mostar ihren Namen.

ically daring lines extending between far-distant shores, towering over the foaming sea.

Bridges always speak in a vivid language of images. Speak romantically from far-eastern gardens and still landscapes, whisper of strollers, loving couples on the bank of the Seine in Paris or the Danube, under the lights of the Chain Bridge in Budapest. And bridges sing with the gondoliers on the lagoons of Venice. Yet these constructions of enchanting arches can also awaken other memories.

The graceful "Bridge of Sighs" in Venice, a covered bridge constructed of white limestone, recalls oppressive times. In the 17th Century, convicts were led over the bridge into incarceration, seeing the light of freedom for the last time for many years, or indeed for ever, as they crossed the lagoon.

The elegant "Stari Most" (Old Bridge) in Bosnia-Herzegovina was for 450 years the most beautiful bridge in the Balkans. It connected trade routes from the Adriatic into the interior of the country. The bridge sentries were called "Mostari" in their local language, giving the name to the town of Mostar. This world-famous monument of Mostar fell victim to the shellfire of the Balkan War in 1993.

This architectural monument, a treasure of the UNESCO World Cultural Heritage, was rebuilt with the aid of international co-operation, and was reconstructed stone by stone. Few building works symbolise so clearly as the bridge of Mostar, as bridges in general, the connecting elements of our cultural heritage and simultaneously the warlike destructiveness of mankind.

"Of everything which man builds and constructs, there is nothing better or more valuable than bridges", wrote the

Malgré tout cela, traverser, franchir un abîme n'a rien perdu de sa magie pour nous. Nous regardons tous avec de grands yeux le paysage qui défile depuis la fenêtre lorsque le train dans lequel nous voyageons franchit des vallées et des montagnes par des viaducs d'une hauteur vertigineuse. Pour la même raison, nous nous hâtons de baisser la fenêtre de notre compartiment, de laisser entrer la fraîche brise marine et d'observer, fascinés, les bateaux qui naviguent au-dessous de nous, par exemple lorsque nous empruntons le majestueux pont d'Öresund entre le Danemark et la Suède, assurément l'un des ouvrages d'ingénierie les plus complexes et les plus grandioses d'Europe. Et quelle magie engendrent les guirlandes de lumière des ponts dans la nuit, les lignes arquées à la surface de l'eau et leur reflet tremblotant et coloré sur les eaux sombres ! Impossible d'effacer de sa mémoire l'impression causée par des ponts tachetés de lumière au-dessus des petits cours d'eau d'une vieille ville aux rues tortueuses, d'un parc pittoresque. Ou la vue de cette courbure audacieuse reliant des rives éloignées, au-dessus d'une mer écumante.

Les ponts nous racontent des histoires dans un langage coloré fait d'une multitude d'images. Leurs récits romantiques parlent souvent de jardins d'Extrême-Orient et de paysages tranquilles. Ils nous chuchotent à l'oreille également des histoires de flâneurs, de couples d'amoureux sur les berges de la Seine à Paris ou du Danube, sous les lumières du pont des chaînes à Budapest. Et les ponts chantent même avec les gondoliers dans les lagunes de Venise ! Mais les merveilleuses arches de ces édifices peuvent également éveiller d'autres souvenirs.

mados la ventanilla al acercarnos a la costa, dejamos que entre la fresca brisa marina y observamos fascinados como los barcos navegan bajo nuestra vía, por ejemplo, al cruzar el majestuoso puente de Öresund, que une Dinamarca y Suecia. Sin duda una de las más complejas y grandiosas edificaciones técnicas de Europa. ¡Y qué cautivadora sensación producen las guirnaldas de luces de los puentes en la oscuridad nocturna! ¡Qué inefable espectáculo forman sus combadas líneas sobre las aguas y su vibrante reflejo multicolor en la oscura corriente! Nadie, que haya contemplado los arcos de puntos relucientes sobre la superficie de uno de esos estrechos cauces urbanos que serpentean a través de un casco antiguo o de un pintoresco parque, podrá borrar de su memoria ese efecto. O la vista de la osada trayectoria esférica con que, a despecho de un mar revuelto y espumeante, quedan comunicadas lejanas orillas.

Los puentes nos narran sus historias en un colorido lenguaje de imágenes.

A menudo sus románticos relatos nos hablan de jardines del extremo oriente y de tranquilos escenarios naturales. También nos susurran al oído sus historias de paseantes: de parejas enamoradas a las orillas del parisino Sena o del Danubio, bajo las luces del puente de las cadenas de Budapest. ¡Y hasta parecen cantar con los gondoleros de las lagunas de Venecia! Y esos no son todos los recuerdos que nos pueden despertar los preciosos arcos de estos edificios.

El veneciano Puente de los Suspiros, que destaca por la indescriptible gracia de su construcción de piedra caliza blanca, nos trae a la memoria episodios opresivos. Sobre este puente eran conducidos a la cárcel en el siglo XVII los con-

un parco pittoresco oppure gli arditi anelli che si allargano tra le rive vicine affacciate sulla schiuma del mare.

I ponti raccontano sempre nella variopinta lingua delle immagini.

Spesso raccontano di romantici giardini del lontano oriente e di paesaggi silenziosi, mormorano di persone a passeggio, di coppie d'innamorati sulle rive della Senna a Parigi o sul Danubio, sotto le luci del ponte delle catene di Budapest o cantano insieme ai gondolieri nella laguna veneziana.

Eppure le costruzioni dagli archi incantati possono risvegliare altri ricordi.

Il grazioso Ponte dei Sospiri a Venezia, realizzato in bianca pietra calcarea ricorda tempi duri. Attraverso questo ponte i condannati venivano condotti in carcere ed attraversando la laguna vedevano per l'ultima volta o non avrebbero visto per lungo tempo la luce della libertà.

L'elegante "Stari Most" (ponte vecchio) in Bosnia-Erzegovina è stato per 450 anni il più bel ponte dei Balcani. Collegava le vie commerciali dal Mar Adriatico all'interno del Paese. Nella lingua locale le sentinelle poste a guardia del ponte si chiamavano "Mostari" e diedero così il nome alla città di Mostar. Nel 1993 il famosissimo monumento di Mostar cadde vittima del fuoco delle granate della guerra dei balcani.

Grazie alla collaborazione internazionale il monumento architettonico, riconosciuto patrimonio dell'umanità dall'UNESCO, poté essere ricostruito, pietra dopo pietra. Poche costruzioni indicano così chiaramente come il ponte di Mostar, e come in generale i ponti, rappresentino il

Das weltbekannte Denkmal von Mostar fiel 1993 dem Granatenfeuer des Balkankrieges zum Opfer.

Das Architekturdenkmal, ein Schatz des Weltkulturerbes der UNESCO, konnte dank internationaler Zusammenarbeit wiederaufgebaut werden, wurde Stein für Stein rekonstruiert. Wenige Bauwerke symbolisieren so deutlich wie die Brücke von Mostar, wie Brücken überhaupt, das Verbindende unseres kulturellen Erbes und gleichzeitig die kriegerische Zerstörungswut des Menschen.

„Von allem, was der Mensch baut und aufbaut, gibt es nichts Besseres und Wertvolleres als Brücken", schrieb der jugoslawische Literaturnobelpreisträger Ivo Andrić (1892–1975). In seinem weltberühmten Roman „Die Brücke über die Drina" erzählt der Schriftsteller die Geschichte des Jahrhunderte alten Bauwerks und damit auch eine Historie der Begegnungen von Orient und Okzident.

Damit Kulturen in Ost und West, Nord und Süd einander näher kommen, einander verstehen lernen, dazu bedurfte und bedarf es des Brückenschlags, architektonisch ebenso wie symbolisch.

In vielerlei Hinsicht sind Brücken ein Mittelpunkt, der vermittelnde Punkt bei Begegnungen, beim Aufeinandertreffen. Die Entwicklung des Verkehrs- und Transportwesens verlangt längst nicht mehr allein nach Überquerung von Wasserläufen, sondern braucht eine Vielzahl von Brücken, um den Verkehrsfluss leiten und bändigen zu können. In dicht besiedelten Regionen, in den Metropolen, beherrschen übereinander führende und ineinander verschlungene Brücken das Bild, sie ermöglichen Autos, Stadtbahnen und Eisenbahnen die ungehinderte Fahrt.

Yugoslavian Nobel Literature Prize-winner Ivo Andrić (1892–1975). In his world-famous novel "The Bridge over the Drina" the author recounts the history of the centuries-old structure, and thus also a history of the meetings between Orient and Occident.

In order for the cultures of East and West, North and South to come closer together, to learn to understand each other, it needed and still needs bridges, both in the architectural and symbolic sense.

In many respects bridges represent the middle point, a point of meeting and of reconciliation. The development of traffic and transport systems has long since required the crossing of many features other than just water, and now needs a variety of bridges in order to direct and control the traffic flow. In densely populated areas, in the major cities, the scene is dominated by bridges leading above and even through each other, enabling cars and trucks, metropolitan railways and long-distance railways to continue their journey unhindered.

The results of utilitarian considerations do not always turn out to be a feast for the eyes. In a peaceful world however, they always fulfil their purpose of enabling people to cover distances more quickly and conveniently, following their compulsion for exchange and new meeting.

Bridges speak of an ancient magic above and beyond the purely technical and cultural aspect. In those arches made not of wood, stone or steel, made up only of water droplets and light, in the rainbow, ancient peoples saw a bridge which connected heaven and earth. Iris, the messenger of the gods, slid down this coloured strand of light to bring

Le Pont des Soupirs à Venise par exemple, cette construction en pierre d'Istrie à la grâce indescriptible, rappelle aussi de tristes épisodes. Au 17ème siècle en effet, ce pont conduisait du tribunal à la prison les condamnés qui soupiraient sachant qu'ils ne reverraient sûrement jamais plus ou pour longtemps la lumière du soleil.
L'élégant «Stari Most» (ou vieux pont en bosniaque) en Bosnie-Herzégovine qui reliait les routes commerciales allant de l'Adriatique vers l'intérieur des terres a été pendant 450 ans le plus beau pont des Balkans. Dans le dialecte local, les gardiens du pont étaient appelés des «mostari» et ce sont donc eux qui ont donné leur nom à la ville de Mostar. Ce monument mondialement célèbre de Mostar est détruit en 1993 par un bombardement au cours de la guerre des Balkans mais, classé sur la liste du patrimoine mondial de l'UNESCO, cet ouvrage architectural a pu être reconstruit pierre par pierre grâce à la coopération internationale. Il existe peu d'ouvrages d'art qui symbolisent aussi clairement que le pont de Mostar, comme les ponts en général, le lien entre le patrimoine culturel commun et la rage destructrice et guerrière des hommes.
«De toutes les choses construites et édifiées par l'homme, il n'est rien de plus beau et de plus précieux que les ponts», a écrit Ivo Andrić (1892–1975), prix Nobel de littérature yougoslave. Dans son célèbre roman «Le pont sur la Drina», l'écrivain raconte l'histoire de cet ouvrage plusieurs fois centenaire et donc l'histoire des rencontres entre l'Orient et l'Occident.
Pour rapprocher les cultures de l'est et de l'ouest, du nord et du sud, pour faire en sorte qu'elles apprennent à se com-denados que, al cruzar la laguna, veían por última vez en mucho tiempo o quizás para siempre la luz de la libertad.
El elegante "Stari Most" (puente viejo) de Bosnia-Herzegovina fue durante 450 años el puente más bello de los Balcanes. Durante todo ese tiempo mantuvo abierta la ruta comercial que conducía desde el Adriático al interior. En el idioma local a los vigilantes del puente se les denominaba "Mostari". Ellos dieron a la ciudad de Mostar su nombre. Aquel mundialmente famoso monumento de Mostar se derrumbó en 1993 bajo el bombardeo de granadas de la guerra de los Balcanes.
Este monumento arquitectónico, un tesoro del Patrimonio de la Humanidad de la UNESCO, pudo ser reconstruido piedra a piedra gracias a la cooperación internacional. Pocas joyas urbanísticas simbolizan tan claramente como el puente de Mostar la función práctica de los puentes en general, el vínculo que supone para los pueblos su patrimonio cultural común así como la sinrazón destructora de la guerra.
"De todas las cosas que los seres humanos construyen y edifican, no hay nada mejor y más valioso que los puentes" escribía el autor yugoslavo y premio Nobel de Literatura Ivo Andrić (1892–1975). En su mundialmente famosa novela "El puente sobre el Drina" el autor narra la historia de este monumento y con ella la historia de los encuentros entre Oriente y Occidente.
Para que se puedan acercar y entender mutuamente las culturas de Oriente y Occidente, del Norte y del Sur, se necesita siempre una cabeza de puente tanto arquitectónica como simbólica.

collegamento con la nostra eredità culturale e contemporaneamente simboleggino la furia distruttrice umana della guerra.
"Di tutto quello che l'uomo costruisce e ricostruisce nulla è migliore e più prezioso dei ponti" scrisse il premio Nobel iugoslavo Ivo Andrić (1892–1975). Nel suo famosissimo romanzo "il ponte sulla Drina" lo scrittore racconta la storia di quella costruzione secolare e quindi anche la storia degli incontri tra oriente ed occidente.
Per avvicinare le culture occidentali ed orientali, il Nord al Sud e facilitarne la reciproca comprensione, serviva e serve tuttora costruire ponti reali ed anche metaforici. Sotto molteplici aspetti i ponti costituiscono elementi di mediazione che si realizzano nel momento dell'incontro e in quello della sovrapposizione delle forze convergenti. Lo sviluppo dei mezzi di trasporto non si limita ormai più all'attraversamento dei corsi d'acqua per poter dirigere ed imbrigliare il flusso del traffico. Nelle regioni ad alta densità di popolazione, nelle metropoli, i ponti sovrapposti ed incrociati tra loro dominano l'immagine e consentono alle automobili, alle ferrovie metropolitane che collegano le grandi città con le aree suburbane e la ferrovia di viaggiare indisturbate.
Non sempre i risultati del pensiero utilitaristico creano opere esteticamente valide. In un mondo pacifico adempiono però sempre la loro funzione di consentire all'uomo di superare in modo più rapido e semplice le distanze nel suo sforzo verso lo scambio e l'incontro.
I ponti raccontano un'antica magia che guarda al collegamento tecnico e culturale. In ogni arco non fatto di legno,

Nicht immer stellen die Ergebnisse des Nützlichkeitsdenkens eine Augenweide dar. In einer friedlichen Welt erfüllen sie jedoch immer ihren Zweck, dass der Mensch schneller, einfacher Distanzen überwinden, seinem Bestreben nach Austausch und Begegnung folgen kann.
Brücken erzählen von einer uralten Magie, welche über die technische und kulturelle Verbindung hinaus weist. In jenen Bögen, die kein Holz, Stein oder Stahl spannt, die nur aus Wassertropfen und Licht bestehen, in den Regenbögen erblickten die Menschen der Frühzeit eine Brücke, die Erde und Himmel miteinander verband. Auf dem farbigen Band glitt die Götterbotin Iris hinab, um den Menschen himmlische Botschaften zu bringen, und auf dem Regenbogen geleitete sie die Verstorbenen ins Himmelreich. Die Priester im alten Rom hießen „Pontifices", der lateinische Wortursprung wird als „Brückenbauer" gedeutet. Bis heute spannt sich diese symbolische Verbindung, indem der Papst den Titel Pontifex Maximus trägt, Oberster Brückenbauer.
Von der zauberhaften Spannung zwischen Kindheitserinnerungen und der Sehnsucht nach dem Unendlichen schrieb Vincent van Gogh. So erzählen Brücken Tausende Geschichten. Viele werden lebendig beim Betrachten der Bilder in diesem Band.

people divine messages, and on the return journey accompanied the dead to the kingdom of heaven. The priests of ancient Rome were called "pontifices", the original Latin word meaning "bridge-builder". This symbolic connection spans the centuries up to the modern day, since one of the titles of the Pope is "Pontifex Maximus" – Supreme bridge-builder.
Vincent van Gogh wrote of the magical tension between childhood memories and longing for the infinite. In the same way, bridges have thousands of stories to tell. Many will come to life when looking at the pictures in this volume.

prendre et à se respecter, il faut toujours jeter des ponts, qu'ils soient concrets ou symboliques.
A de nombreux égards, les ponts peuvent former un point central, le point médiateur lors de contacts et de rencontres. L'évolution des transports en général est telle qu'elle n'exige plus depuis longtemps uniquement de pouvoir traverser des cours d'eau. Aujourd'hui, il faut construire de nombreux ponts afin de guider le flux des véhicules et de pouvoir le maîtriser. Dans les régions densément peuplées, dans les métropoles, le paysage urbain est dominé par un entrelacement de ponts qui permettent aux voitures, aux métros et aux trains de circuler sans problème.
Les ponts racontent des histoires d'une magie venue du fond des temps, qui va bien au-delà d'un lien technique et culturel. Ces arcs-en-ciel étaient autrefois considérés par les hommes comme un pont reliant le ciel et la terre. Iris, messagère ailée des Dieux, descendait autrefois sur cet arc lumineux coloré pour apporter des messages célestes à l'humanité et accompagner les défunts jusque dans le royaume des cieux. Les prêtres de l'ancienne Rome portaient le titre de «pontifices» qui signifie en latin «bâtisseur de ponts». Jusqu'à aujourd'hui, ce lien symbolique persiste car le pape est le Pontifex Maximus ou maître bâtisseur de ponts.
Vincent van Gogh a écrit sur l'arc de tension magique entre les souvenirs d'enfance et la nostalgie de l'infini. Les ponts racontent des milliers d'histoires dont certaines prennent vie lorsque l'on contemple les photos réunies dans cet ouvrage.

Desde muchos puntos de vista los puentes son un nexo, el punto de transmisión de encuentros y encontronazos. El desarrollo del tráfico y el transporte no sólo exige la superación de cauces, sino que también requiere una gran cantidad de tipos de puentes destinados a distribuir y controlar los flujos circulatorios. Tanto en las regiones densamente pobladas como en las metrópolis, el panorama está dominado por gigantescos enlaces elevados de carreteras de complejas formas. Estas construcciones hacen posible la circulación del tráfico así como la confluencia de carreteras y autopistas urbanas con las líneas ferroviarias.
Los puentes son mudos testigos de una antiquísima magia que va más allá del mero establecimiento de comunicación técnica e intercultural. Ya en el arcoiris –en ese arco que no está hecho de madera, piedra o acero, sino de gotas de agua y luz– veían nuestros antepasados prehistóricos una conexión entre el cielo y la tierra. Por su cinta multicolor descendía Iris, la mensajera de los dioses, para trasladar a los humanos mensajes celestiales. Y sobre esa misma banda acompañaba a los fallecidos al Reino de las Alturas. Los sacerdotes de la antigua Roma se denominaban "pontífices", una palabra cuyo significado original se interpreta como "constructores de puentes". Hasta hoy en día llega esa simbólica conexión, pues el Papa lleva el título de "Pontifex Maximus". Es decir, "máximo constructor de puentes".
Vincent van Gogh escribía sobre la mágica conexión que existe entre los recuerdos de la infancia y el ansia de eternidad. También los puentes nos cuentan miles de esas historias trascendentales. Muchas de ellas se convertirán para Vd. en memoria viva al contemplar las ilustraciones de este tomo.

pietra o acciaio ma soltanto di gocce d'acqua, luce ed arcobaleno gli uomini vedono l'abbozzo di un ponte che collega terra e cielo. Sul nastro colorato scivola la messaggera degli dei Iride per portare agli uomini messaggi divini. Sull'arcobaleno conduceva i morti nel Regno dei Cieli. I sacerdoti dell'antica Roma si chiamavano "pontefici", che secondo l'etimologia latina significa "costruttori di ponti". Fino ad oggi si protrae questo legame simbolico che attribuisce al Papa il titolo di Pontefice Massimo, il sommo costruttore di ponti.
Vincent Van Gogh descrisse la magica tensione tra i ricordi dell'infanzia e la nostalgia dell'infinito, ma anche i ponti sanno raccontare migliaia di storie. E molte prendono vita osservando le immagini di quest'opera.

1 Brooklyn Bridge & Manhattan Bridge, New York, USA
2 Fred Hartman Bridge, Houston, USA
3 George Washington Bridge, New York, USA
4 Queensboro Bridge, New York, USA
5 San Francisco–Oakland Bay Bridge, San Francisco, USA
6 Vicksburg Bridge, Vicksburg, USA
7 Yaquina Bay Bridge, Newport, USA
8 Viaducto La Polvorilla, Tren a las Nubes, Argentina
9 Puente, Chiu Chiu, Chile
10 Belgacom, Bruxelles, Belgique
11 Pont de Wandre, Herstal, Belgique
12 Storebæltsbroerne, Fünen–Zeeland, Danmark
13 Dronning Alexandrines Bro, Kalvehave, Danmark
14 Elbbrücke, Hamburg, Deutschland
15 Götzschtal Viadukt, Mylau, Deutschland
16 Hohenzollernbrücke, Köln, Deutschland
17 Seebrücke, Sellin, Deutschland
18 Docklands, London, England
19 Palace Pier, Brighton, England
20 Tower Bridge, London, England
21 Puente de Plaza de España, Sevilla, España
22 Puente del Alamillo, Sevilla, España
23 Puente Fortificado, Besalú, España
24 Pont Neuf, Paris, France
25 Tour Pacific, Paris, France
26 Viaduc du Garabit, St. Flour, France
27 Ponte della Maddalena, Borgo a Mozzano, Italia
28 Ponte Vecchio, Firenze, Italia
29 Széchenyi Lánchíd, Budapest, Magyarország
30 Erasmusbrug, Rotterdam, Nederlands
31 Ponte Dom Luís I., Porto, Portugal
32 Puente Vasco da Gama, Lisboa, Portugal
33 Firth of Forth Bridge, Edinburgh, Scotland
34 Tay Bridge, Dundee, Scotland
35 Galata Köprüsü, Istanbul, Türkiye
36 Köprü, Çine, Türkiye
37 Changjiang Daqiao, Nanjing, China
38 Changjiang Daqiao, Wuhan, China
39 Lugouqiao, Beijing, China
40 Ponte de Amizade, Macao, China
41 Tiananmen Square, Beijing, China
42 Ting Kau Bridge, Hong Kong, China
43 Shiqikongqiao, Beijing, China
44 Akashi-Kaikyo Bashi, Kobe, Japan
45 Heian Jingu, Kyoto, Japan
46 Kazura Bashi, Oboke, Japan
47 Kintai-Kyo Bashi, Iwakuni, Japan
48 Shimotsui-Seto, Kojima, Japan
49 Umeda Sky Building, Osaka, Japan
50 Sydney Harbour Bridge, Sydney, Australia

1 Brooklyn Bridge & Manhattan Bridge, New York, USA

2 Fred Hartman Bridge, Houston, USA

► 3 George Washington Bridge, New York, USA

9A
SOUTH
Downtown
SOUTH
Downtown
NORTH
Upstate
Riverside Dr
SPEED
LIMIT
30

4 Queensboro Bridge, New York, USA

5 San Francisco–Oakland Bay Bridge, San Francisco, USA

6 Vicksburg Bridge, Vicksburg, USA

AMERISTAR
CASINO

7 Yaquina Bay Bridge, Newport, USA

8 Viaducto La Polvorilla, Tren a las Nubes, Argentina

► 9 Puente, Chiu Chiu, Chile

10 Belgacom, Bruxelles, Belgique

11 Pont de Wandre, Herstal, Belgique

12 Storebæltsbroerne, Fünen–Zeeland, Danmark

13 Dronning Alexandrines Bro, Kalvehave, Danmark

14 Elbbrücke, Hamburg, Deutschland

► **15** Göltzschtal Viadukt, Mylau, Deutschland

16 Hohenzollernbrücke, Köln, Deutschland

17 Seebrücke, Sellin, Deutschland

18 Docklands, London, England

► **19** Palace Pier, Brighton, England

PALACE PIER
PALACE PIER
KIDS RIDES CORNER

20 Tower Bridge, London, England

21 Puente de Plaza de España, Sevilla, España

22 Puente del Alamillo, Sevilla, España

23 Puente Fortificado, Besalú, España

24 Pont Neuf, Paris, France

► **25** Tour Pacific, Paris, France

26 Viaduc du Garabit, St. Flour, France

27 Ponte della Maddalena, Borgo a Mozzano, Italia

28 Ponte Vecchio, Firenze, Italia

► **29** Széchenyi Lánchíd, Budapest, Magyarország

RÁKÓCZI

30 Erasmusbrug, Rotterdam, Nederlands

31 Ponte Dom Luís I., Porto, Portugal

► **32** Puente Vasco da Gama, Lisboa, Portugal

33 Firth of Forth Bridge, Edinburgh, Scotland

34 Tay Bridge, Dundee, Scotland

35 Galata Köprüsü, Istanbul, Türkiye

► **36** Köprü, Çine, Türkiye

37 Changjiang Daqiao, Nanjing, China

38 Changjiang Daqiao, Wuhan, China

39 Lugouqiao, Beijing, China

40 Ponte de Amizade, Macao, China

41 Tiananmen Square, Beijing, China

► **42** Ting Kau Bridge, Hong Kong, China

COSCO

43 Shiqikongqiao, Beijing, China

► **44** Akashi-Kaikyo Bashi, Kobe, Japan

45 Heian Jingu, Kyoto, Japan

46 Kazura Bashi, Oboke, Japan

47 Kintai-Kyo Bashi, Iwakuni, Japan

48 Shimotsui-Seto, Kojima, Japan

49 Umeda Sky Building, Osaka, Japan

► **50** Sydney Harbour Bridge, Sydney, Australia

AMP
AMP

NO
STANDING

KARL LANG wurde 1932 in Duisburg geboren. Nach der Ausbildung zum Industrie- und Werbephotograph arbeitete er für verschiedene Bildagenturen. Von 1965 bis 1993 leitete er die Photoabteilung der Thyssen Unternehmensgruppe. 1985 gründete er das eigene Photostudio in Essen, das sich auf Industriephotographie spezialisierte. Seine Reisen führten ihn auf alle Kontinente dieser Erde, seine Aufnahmen wurden vielfach ausgestellt und u. a. in Turin, Hongkong, Newcastle, Fribourg und Johannesburg prämiert. Karl Lang wurde im Jahr 2000 für seine Photoserie „Bridges“ mit dem renommierten World Press Photo Award ausgezeichnet.

IMRE TÖRÖK ist gebürtiger Ungar und kam als Jugendlicher nach Deutschland. Nach dem Erlernen der deutschen Sprache absolvierte er ein Studium der Germanistik, Geschichte und Philosophie in Tübingen, wo er Schüler von Ernst Bloch war. Imre Török ist Bundesvorsitzender des Verbands deutscher Schriftsteller (VS), Mitglied im P.E.N.-Zentrum Deutschland und des ungarischen Schriftstellerverbands. Er hat als Dozent, Journalist und Leiter eines städtischen Theaters gearbeitet. Seit Langem ist er als freier Schriftsteller und Kultur-Arbeiter tätig. Imre Töröks Werk umfasst Kurzgeschichten, Romane, Märchen, poetische Prosa und Sachbücher. Neben seinen zahlreichen Buchveröffentlichungen hat er auch am Kinofilm „Sophie Scholl. Die letzten Tage“ mitgearbeitet.

KARL LANG was born in 1932 in Duisburg. After his training as industrial and commercial photographer he worked for several Photo Agencies. From 1965 to 1993 he was head of the photo department of the Thyssen group. In 1985 he established his own photo studio in Essen, which specialized in industrial photography. He travelled widely on all continents of the earth and his images were exhibited many times and at many places such as Turin, Hong Kong, Newcastle, Fribourg and Johannesburg, where they also received awards. For his photo series "Bridges", Karl Lang received the renowned World Press Photo Award in the year 2000.

IMRE TÖRÖK came to Germany as a boy after being born in Hungary. After learning to speak German, he studied German language, history and philosophy in Tübingen, where he was a pupil of Ernst Bloch. Imre Török is the National Chairman of the "Verband deutscher Schriftsteller" (VS), and a member of the "P.E.N.-Zentrum Deutschland" and the Hungarian Writers' Association. He has worked as a lecturer, journalist and director of a municipal theatre. For many years now, he has worked as a freelance author and cultural worker. Imre Török's work includes short stories, novels, fairytales, poetic prose and non-fiction. In addition to his many book publications, he also co-operated on the film "Sophie Scholl. Die letzten Tage".

KARL LANG est né en 1932 à Duisbourg. Après une formation de photographe industriel et publicitaire, il travaille pour différentes agences. De 1965 à 1993, il dirige le service de photographie du groupe d'entreprises Thyssen. Il fonde en 1985 son propre studio de photographie à Essen, qui se spécialise dans la photographie industrielle. Ses voyages le menent sur tous les continents, ses travaux sont exposés à de nombreuses reprises et notamment primés à Turin, Hongkong, Newcastle, Fribourg et Johannesburg. Karl Lang obtient en 2000 pour sa série de photographies « Bridges » la célèbre distinction World Press Photo Award.

IMRE TÖRÖK, né en Hongrie, est arrivé en Allemagne à l'âge de l'adolescence. Après avoir appris la langue, il fait des études de philologie allemande, d'histoire et de philosophie à Tübingen, où il est l'élève d'Ernst Bloch. Imre Török est le président national du «Verband deutscher Schrifsteller (VS)» ainsi que membre du «P.E.N.-Zentrum Deutschland» et de l'association hongroise des écrivains. Il a été professeur, journaliste et directeur d'un théâtre municipal. Il est depuis longtemps écrivain libre et professionnel de la culture. Imre Török a écrit des nouvelles, des romans, des contes, de la prose poétique ainsi que des livres d'essai. Outre de nombreuses publications livresques, il a également travaillé sur le film de cinéma «Sophie Scholl. Les derniers jours.»

KARL LANG nació en 1932 en Duisburg (Alemania). Tras concluir su formación de fotógrafo publicitario e industrial trabajó para diversas agencias de fotografía. Entre 1965 y 1993 dirigió el departamento de fotografía del consorcio empresarial Thyssen. En 1985 fundó su propio estudio dedicado a la fotografía industrial en Essen. Él ha celebrado varias exposiciones dedicadas a las fotografías que ha realizado durante sus viajes por todos los continentes. Sus obras han sido premiadas en diversos eventos realizados en Turin, Hongkong, Newcastle, Friburgo y Johannesburgo. En 2000 Karl Lang fue galardonado con el prestigioso premio "World Press Photo Award" por su serie fotográfica "Bridges".

IMRE TÖRÖK es oriundo de Hungría y vino a Alemania cuando todavía era un adolescente. Tras haber aprendido el idioma alemán realizó las carreras de Filología Germánica, Historia y Filosofía en Tübingen, donde fue alumno de Ernst Bloch. Imre Török es presidente de la Asociación de Escritores Alemanes (VS), miembro del centro P.E.N. de Alemania así como de la Asociación de Escritores Húngaros. Él ha trabajado como docente, periodista y director de un teatro municipal. Desde hace mucho tiempo trabaja como escritor independiente y creador de cultura. La amplia obra de Imre Töröks abarca narraciones breves, novelas, cuentos, prosa poética y libros de divulgación. Entre la edición de sus muchas publicaciones, Imre Török también colaboró en la confección de la película "Los últimos días de Sophie Scholl".

KARL LANG è nato nel 1932 a Duisburg. Dopo un corso di formazione a fotografo industriale e pubblicitario lavorò per diverse agenzie fotografiche. Dal 1965 al 1993 egli diresse il reparto di fotografia del Gruppo imprenditoriale Thyssen. Nel 1985 fondò il proprio studio fotografico a Essen, specializzandosi in fotografia industriale. I suoi viaggi lo hanno portato in tutti i continenti di questo pianeta, le sue immagini sono state esposte in molte località e premiate tra l'altro a Torino, Hongkong, Newcastle, Friburgo e Johannesburg. Nel 2000 è stato conferito a Karl Lang per la sue serie di fotografie "Bridges" il rinomato World Press Photo Award.

IMRE TÖRÖL è nato in Ungheria e arrivò da ragazzo in Germania. Dopo aver appreso la lingua tedesca si laureò in Germanistica, Storia e Filosofia a Tubinga dove fu allievo di Ernst Bloch. Imre Török è presidente federale dell'Associazione Scrittori Tedeschi (VS), membro del centro P.E.N. in Germania e dell'Associazione Scrittori Ungheresi. Ha lavorato come docente, giornalista e direttore di un teatro cittadino. Da molto tempo è attivo come libero scrittore ed intellettuale. Le opere di Imre Töröks comprendono racconti brevi, romanzi, fiabe, prosa poetica e testi di saggistica. Oltre alle numerose pubblicazioni d'opere ha collaborato anche al lavoro cinematografico "Sophie Scholl. Gli ultimi giorni".

ISBN: 978-3-89823-336-1

Concept: Bernhard Wipfler, Sebastian Wipfler, Marcus Bela Schmitt
Design: EDITION PANORAMA | Diana May and Designgruppe Fanz & Neumayer | Marcus Bela Schmitt
Editorial department: Dr. Michael Barchet, Wolfgang Roth
Translations: Global-Text Fachübersetzungen, Heidelberg | Mark Woolfe, Jocelyne Abarca, Dr. Maria Carasi, Sebastián González Mohíno
Separations: EPS GmbH, Speyer
Printing: abcdruck GmbH, Heidelberg
Bookbinding: Josef Spinner Großbuchbinderei GmbH, Ottersweier

EDITION PANORAMA GmbH
G7, 14
D-68159 Mannheim

www.editionpanorama.com

A production by EDITION**PANORAMA**

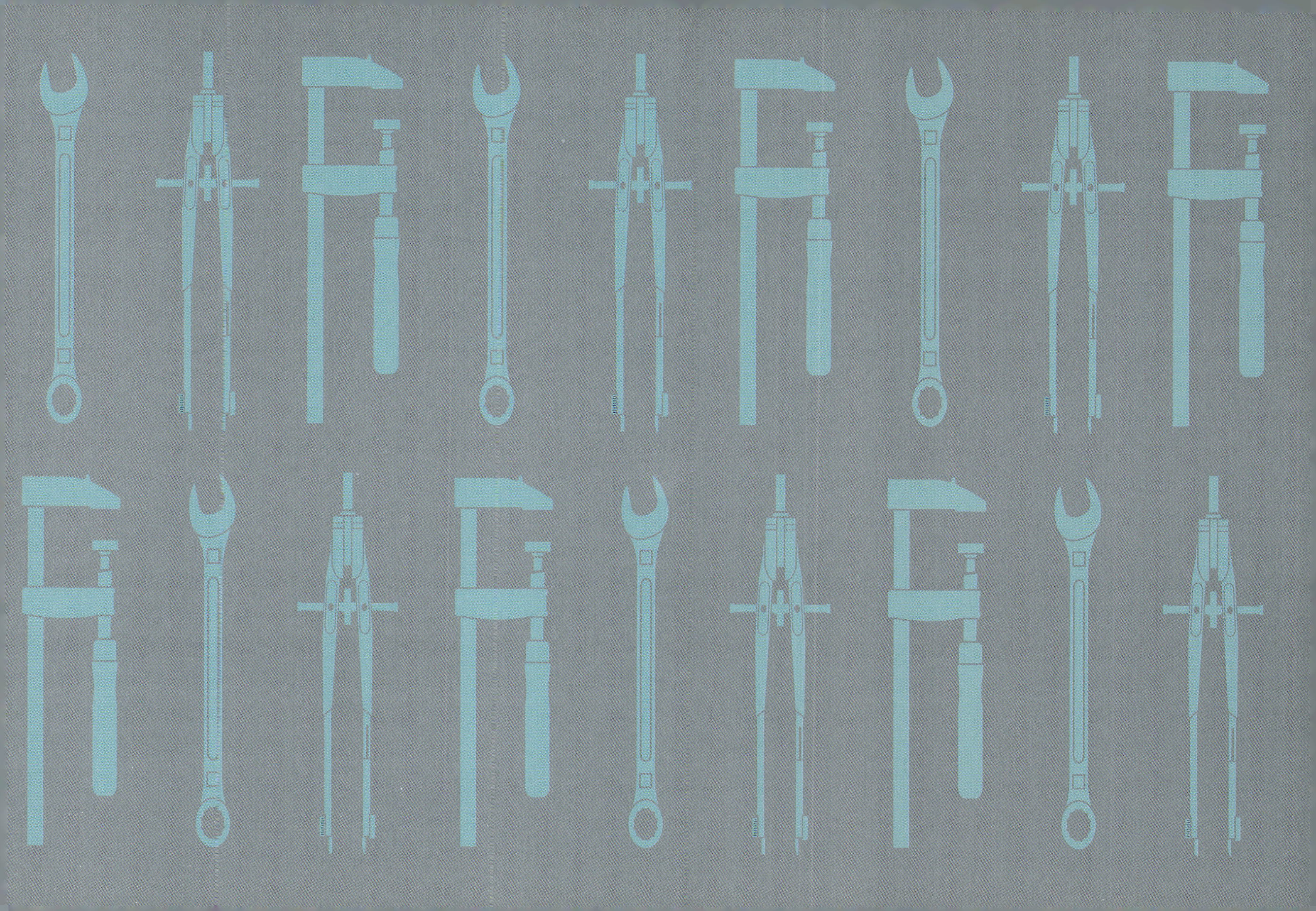

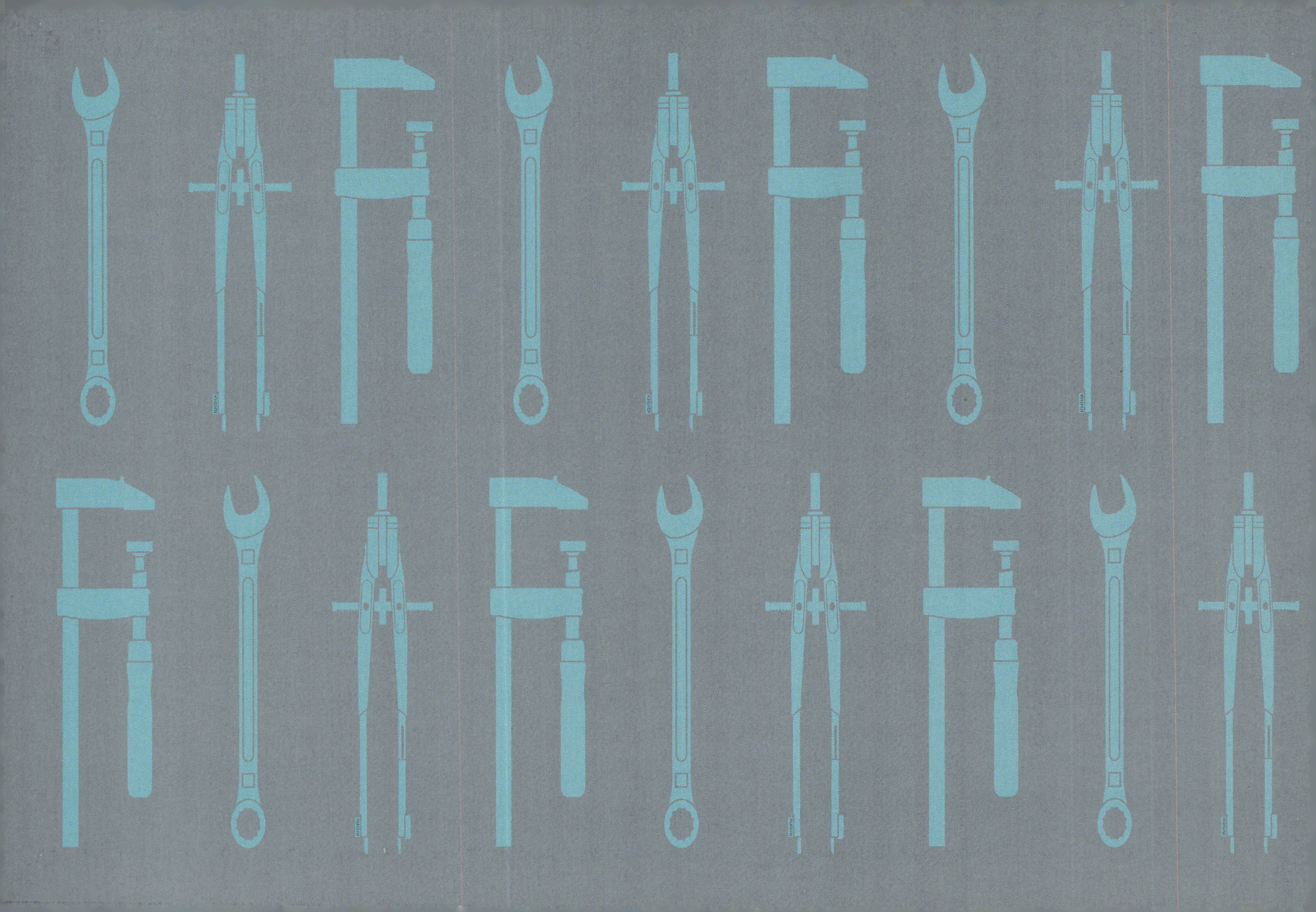